This book belongs to:

_____

Published by the division of Deeper Revelation Books devoted to topics that concern social issues and success in life:
PIVOTAL PUBLICATIONS
Relevant truth for pivotal change

P.O. Box 4260, Cleveland, TN 37320
Phone: 423-478-2843
Email: *info@deeperrevelationbooks.org*
Website: *www.deeperrevelationbooks.org*

Deeper Revelation Books and its divisions assist Christian writers in publishing and distributing their works. Our authors are the ultimate decision-makers in the process. Final responsibility for the creative design, content, permissions, editorial accuracy, stories and doctrinal views, either expressed or implied, belongs to the author. What you hold in your hand is an expression of this author's passion to publish the truth to this generation with a spirit of excellence. It was a blessing and an honor to assist in this process.

FOREWORD

I have had a very interesting and fulfilling career as a teacher, coach, and high school principal. Experiencing the joy of seeing my students learn and excel in life has been very rewarding. NFL Hall of Famer, Reggie White, was one of my most notable high school students. He realized his education could take him to prominent places of purpose and influence. He became a college student-athlete, a professional all-star football player, a minister of the Gospel and author of eight books.

Venus Lacy was one of my students with a learning disability. I was able to convince her that she could learn and that education was the key to her success. Venus began to study as hard as she played basketball. She went on to become a successful college student-athlete who led Louisiana Tech to a national championship. She was also a 1996 Olympic Gold Medalist for the U.S. Women's Basketball Team, and she played several years in the WNBA. She is in the process of writing her book.

Mentoring students like Reggie and Venus gives me great joy and inspiration to continue teaching. I was inspired by my teachers to pursue my dreams through education at Howard School in Chattanooga, Tennessee. However, after reading about the amazing story of Mary Walker, who learned how to read, write, and do math at 117 years old, my inspiration for learning has increased ten-fold. Her motivation for learning to read was fueled by her desire to read the Bible. Her story has inspired me as an educator to help her legacy to live on by awakening the same desire in others. "You are never too old to learn," said Mary. I am echoing that motivational message to all who feel, for one reason or another, that education is something they could never attain.

The Mary Walker Foundation is on a mission to alleviate poverty, develop people's full potential, create love for God, love for others, and love for knowledge through literacy and education. A prophet in the Old Testament said it so well—"My people are destroyed for the lack of knowledge" (Hosea 4:6). We are doing all we can to steer people away from that unfortunate outcome, and find success in life instead.

KNOWLEDGE IS POWERFUL AND DIVINE! JOIN THE MOVEMENT!

— Lurone "Coach" Jennings, Sr., Chairman of the Board

Mary Walker was born in 1848, in Union Springs, a little town in Alabama. She was born an enslaved child to parents who were also enslaved. They were surrounded by the cotton fields that they worked in every day. Her life was much different than other little children. Reading and writing were not allowed for her people. But that didn't stop Mary from dreaming that one day she would be able to read a book, write a letter, or even sign her own name. She would listen to her parents and others talk about freedom. She would often think, "What is that? What does it mean to be free?" The answer to those questions was not far off.

Liberty came about fifteen years later for Mary and her family. Abraham Lincoln was the President of the United States at that time. He signed a document called "The Emancipation Proclamation" on January 1, 1863. It declared that the enslaved people in the Southern states were no longer bound to their former life. The Proclamation granted freedom for 3.1 million enslaved persons. The Emancipation was a giant on paper, but a ghost in reality—because in many ways life did not improve. Mary was fourteen when freedom came. But did it? Former enslaved people had nothing. They were not able to read or write. They couldn't find jobs in the South. Many chose to go north on the Freedom Road. Mary and her family chose to stay in Alabama. Freedom came with a price. It was better, but it was not easy.

4

Life was difficult in many ways, but Mary made the best of it. She worked hard for very small wages. Always with a smile on her face and a song in her heart, Mary was delighted to be alive. She was excited and thankful to be free. Everyone loved Mary. Hard knocks had not made her bitter or angry. No, quite the opposite. All the challenges she faced made her stronger and more loving. She always tried to look for the best in people. She believed that there was a better life to be had.

One day, a minister friend gave her a special book. It was large and had a lot of writing in it. She didn't know how to say the words or what they meant, but that book became very dear to her. She cherished it. It was the first book that Mary had ever owned. This book would go with her till the end of her days and one day she would know what it said. She promised herself, "Someday, I will learn to read and write."

Mary did not waste any time pursuing what would become a full and eventful life. She refused to be discouraged or hindered by the lingering segregation and racism of the times. By the age of twenty, she was married and had her first child. Mary worked hard to support her growing family. Jobs were not easy to come by for someone that could neither read nor write. She worked in the field. She was a housekeeper, a cleaning woman, and a babysitter. There was no job too small for her. Determination was her constant companion. She was a brave woman, willing to do whatever it took to be the best mother, wife, and friend she could be. One of her greatest joys was going to church and learning about the wonderful stories that were in the book that she owned, but still could not read.

8

It was time for a change. The family decided to move to Chattanooga, Tennessee, in 1917 because the city was growing so fast. Mary was sixty-eight years old, a mother of three, longing to give her boys a better life.

Unfortunately, that was year of the Great Flood. The water level rose forty-seven feet above normal, sweeping away almost everything in its path. Devastation was everywhere. It was a very sad and painful time. But as soon as the flood was over, reconstruction began. The timing of the 1917 flood also coincided with the completion of the Market Street Bridge, which is still in Chattanooga to this day.

Mary understood, by this stage of her life, that times of great crisis can become times of great opportunity. Even with the challenges that came, she was thrilled with this move, leaving the old behind and embracing a fresh start—for her and for her family.

One, two, three. That is how many sons Mary had. Each time a child was born, Mary had someone write the new baby's name and birthday in her big book, the one she had carried with her and treasured for many years. Even though she could not read or write, she wanted to have a record of when her boys were born. Mary didn't know when it would happen, but one day, she was sure that she would learn to read and write. She felt that opportunities would open up for her once she succeeded in reaching that goal. She never could have imagined how great those opportunities would be.

Three, two, one, zero. That's how many sons Mary had left. One by one, all three of her sons and her husband passed away. Mary found herself all alone for the first time in her life. Some people who knew about Mary discovered that she was the oldest, surviving person in the United States who was formerly enslaved. Mary was thankful for that. But even though she was free from the unjust institution of slavery, she became enslaved to time. Mary had more than enough time to constantly think about her losses in the past, her challenges in the present, and what she might face in the future. What would Mary do? She didn't know it, but great things were about to happen for her.

When one door closes, another one will open. Mary needed a door to open for her, and it certainly did. She moved into a retirement center. It was there that she made new friends and found a renewed desire to read and write. Her new home was always busy. People coming and going. Laughter filled the air of the apartment building. That was so refreshing. Mary could share with others her interests in cooking and bonnet making. But most importantly, she joined CALM (Chattanooga Area Literacy Movement). When twenty-six people walked into a classroom intending to learn how to read and write, Mary Walker was one of them. As you can imagine, her jaws were almost sore from smiling so big.

Nation's Oldest
Student
Is presented to:
Mary Walker

The "prize pupil" award went to Grandma Mary Walker. When she walked into the classroom, she couldn't read or write. But she applied herself daily, intending to excel. Though frustrated at times, she refused to be a quitter. Her determination and happiness were a winning combination. Not only was she the oldest citizen in the United States, she became the nation's oldest student. In fact, she was certified as "The Nation's Oldest Student" by the U.S. Department of Health, Education, and Welfare.

When she would rest in her home, she would often look over at her beloved Bible, the book that had traveled with her for over a hundred years. Then she would speak to it out loud, and declare, "You hold on, precious book. Soon I'm going to read you from cover to cover." And that's exactly what she did. Finally, Mary could read, and Mary could write.

18

It took Mary Walker at least a hundred years to become a "celebrity." But she was a fine one. She gained national attention by learning to read and write at her age. One of her favorite sayings was, "You are never too old to learn." She was celebrated by presidents, senators, governors, mayors and so many more people and organizations. She was even given the key to the city of Chattanooga and was named an "Ambassador of Goodwill." At a birthday party, she demonstrated her newfound ability by reading from a small pamphlet titled, "What's on the Moon?" She spoke in a clear and strong voice and did not miss a single word. That amazing achievement brought a round of applause from her admiring audience.

MARY WALKER TOWERS

20

What adventure would Mary tackle next? She believed that life is a gift, and that no one should ever stop growing and learning. There is always something new to experience. You don't get Mary's age without learning that lesson. "So, what should I do now?" Mary thought. "Why not go on my very first plane ride?"

The pilot tried to help her into the cockpit, but feisty Mary said, "I got it." Once settled, she reached out and grasped the co-pilot's controls and broke into a wide grin. She was thinking, "I learned to read and write. Maybe being a pilot won't be that hard." They flew over her the apartment building where she lived. Her friends waved and Mary waved back. They flew up above Lookout Mountain. How exciting! Was Mary afraid? Absolutely not!

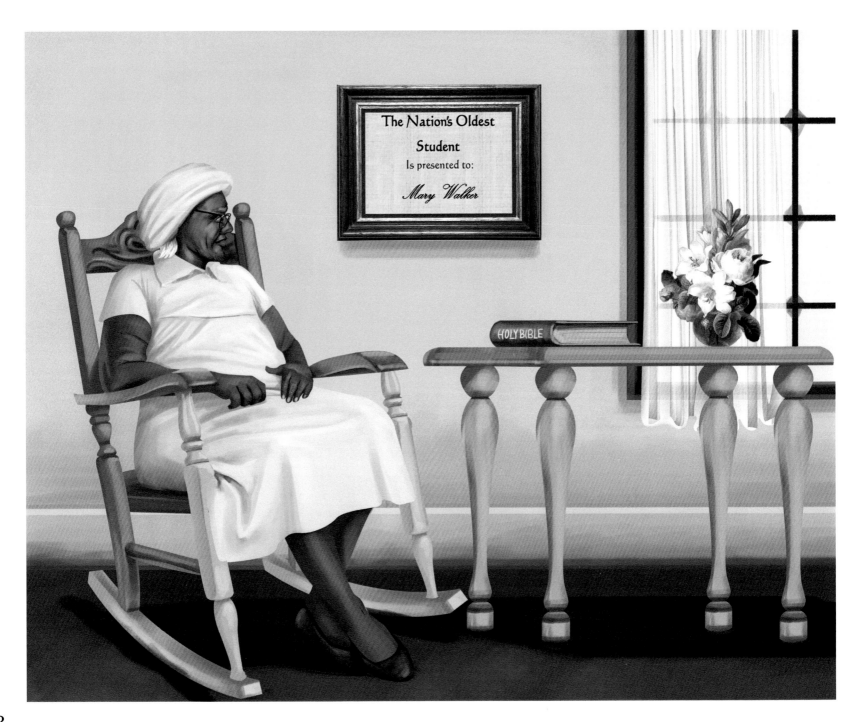

After all the celebrations were over, Mary went to Room 313 at the High Rise Apartments. She sat down in her rocking chair with a perfect view of the sky. "Blessed beyond all measure" is how she felt. Her trusted companion sat right there on the table next to her. How quickly time had passed! Mary shook her head, amazed that it had been over a hundred years since she was gifted this beautiful treasure. The book cover was beginning to look tattered. The handwriting inside was beginning to fade. But her lifelong goal had finally been reached. Mary could read from her beloved book—the Bible. Its words became more inspiring to her than ever before.

Even though Mary, at times, had to endure hardship, she always tried to express a rare but valuable quality called "Gratitude"—both to God and to people. She was one of the kindest ladies you would ever meet, so full of appreciation for whatever blessing she received from God through people.

Mary lived under twenty-six Presidents. She lived through six major wars in the United States, including the Civil War, World War I, World War II, and the Vietnam War. She saw quite a few natural disasters—like tornados, hailstorms, and floods—come and go. She birthed three sons and buried three sons. Her life was a roller coaster of happiness and sadness. But one thing for certain, her faith in God and in humanity never wavered.

2A 73

MARY WALKER
—1848-1969—

Born a slave in Union Springs, Alabama, "Grandma" Walker moved to Chattanooga in 1917 and remained here until her death. At the age of 116 she enrolled in the Chattanooga Area Literacy Movement class and learned to read, write, and solve arithmetic problems. She twice received Chattanooga's Ambassador of Goodwill award and was declared the oldest student in the nation by the U. S. Department of Health, Education, and Welfare.

TENNESSEE HISTORICAL COMMISSION

Mary had no idea how inspiring her journey would be to others. She never attempted to promote herself; she just tried to live as good and decent as she could. But actions always speak louder than words and people took note.

The door of her earthly journey finally closed when she was one-hundred-and twenty-one years and seven months old. But her remarkable age was not the most important aspect of who she was. What she did, the way she did it, and the time in which it was done were all important factors. All those things set her apart and made her life an extraordinary beacon of light that would illuminate the path so others could follow. What an amazing legacy she left behind!

The City of Chattanooga renamed her former retirement home in her honor. It is now called Mary Walker Towers. They also created a memorial that can be found at 3031 Wilcox Blvd. In 1970, Chattanooga's Mary Walker Foundation was established to promote academic and economic literacy in the city through reading and writing classes, historical displays, family crisis support, and scholarships. You should go and visit someday, because now, it's your turn to shine.

The inspiring example of Mary Walker's life still has the power to make a sinner a saint, produce love out of hate, awaken goodness out of evil, help honesty overcome lies, cause light to shine out of darkness, and raise the banner of freedom over all the things that enslave human beings. The testimony of her accomplishments will surely cause literacy to rise out of the ashes of illiteracy for many years to come.

There is faith in her story. There is hope in her story. There is love in her story. Yes—faith, hope, and love—these are precious things we all desperately need. So, how do we sum up this account of the amazing Mary Walker? Not only was she the oldest, living, formerly enslaved person and the oldest, living student, she was and still is a valuable role model. Her journey encourages all of us to make the best of our lives by reaching for the highest possible goals—even some that, at first, appear almost impossible.

Reverend J. Lloyd Edwards Jr.

At 90 years old, Reverend John Lloyd Edwards was one of Chattanooga's oldest and most active ministers, pastoring Cosmopolitan Community Church. He was born to The Late Reverend John Lloyd Edwards, Sr. and Mahala Edwards in Oklahoma City, Oklahoma, as the second youngest of twelve children. Several communities in Oklahoma are named after the Edwards family, who were early pioneers in the state's Black community.

**Reverend
J. Lloyd Edwards Jr.**

Reverend Edwards is the author of *Ex-Slave Extra: The Mary Walker Story* and is regarded as one of the region's major proponents of literacy and Black History. That was the original book used as the primary source for the information contained in this account titled, *The Amazing Mary Walker*.

THE MARY WALKER FOUNDATION

Mary Walker

The Mary Walker Foundation promotes economic literacy and stability for all through reading, writing, and education. Our mission is to help alleviate poverty for all Chattanooga citizens and help create economic stability through literacy training and educational activities.

"My people are destroyed for lack of knowledge." (Hosea 4:6 KJV)

"Wisdom and knowledge will be the stability of your times, and the strength of salvation." (Isaiah 33:6 NKJV)

For more information on Mary Walker and the foundation

Visit our website: www.marywalkerfoundation.org
Call the foundation: 423-267-2313
Email us: info@MaryWalkerFoundation.org
Mail: The Mary Walker Foundation
611 East M.L. King Blvd.
Chattanooga, TN 37403